As *your* Redemption

To Include:

As *your* Righteousness
As *your* Sanctification
As *your* Strength
As *your* Wisdom

Andrew Murray

As *your* Redemption

Of God are ye in Christ Jesus, who was made unto us wisdom from God, both righteousness and sanctification, and redemption.[1]

H ere we have the top of the ladder, reaching into heaven – the blessed end to which Christ and life in Him is to lead. The word redemption, though sometimes applied to our deliverance from the guilt of sin, here refers to our complete and final deliverance from all its consequences, when the Redeemer's work shall become fully manifest, even to the redemption of the body itself.[2] The expression points us to the highest glory to be hoped for in the future, and therefore also to the highest blessing to be enjoyed in the present in Christ. We have seen how, as a Prophet, Christ is our wisdom, revealing to us God and His love, with the nature and conditions of the salvation that love has prepared. As a Priest, He is our righteousness, restoring us to right relations to God, and securing us His favor and friendship. As a King, He is our sanctification, forming and guiding us into the obedience to the Father's holy will. As these three offices work out God's one purpose, the grand consummation will be reached, the complete deliverance from sin and all its effects be accomplished, and ransomed humanity regain all that it had ever lost.

Christ is made of God unto us redemption. The word invites us to look upon Jesus, not only as He lived on earth, teaching us by word and example, as He died, to reconcile us with God, as He lives again, a victorious King, rising to receive His crown, but as, sitting at the right hand of God, He takes again the glory which He had with the Father, before the world began, and holds it there for us. It consists in this, that there His human nature, yea, His human body, freed from all the consequences of sin to which He once had been exposed, is now admitted to share the divine glory. As Son of Man, He dwells on the throne and in the bosom of the Father: the deliverance from what He had to suffer from

---

[1] *1 Cor.1:30 -*

[2] *Rom.8: 21-23; Eph.1.14; 4:30 -*

sin is complete and eternal. The complete redemption is found embodied in His own Person: what He as man is and has in heaven is the complete redemption. HE is made of God to us redemption.

We are in Him as such. And the more intelligently and believingly we abide in Him as our redemption, the more shall we experience, even here, of "the powers of the world to come." As our communion with Him becomes more intimate and intense, and we let the Holy Spirit reveal Him to us in His heavenly glory, the more we realize how the life in us is the life of One who sits upon the throne of heaven. We feel the power of an endless life working in us. We taste the eternal life. We have the foretaste of the eternal glory.

The blessings flowing from abiding in Christ as our redemption are great. The soul is delivered from all fear of death. There was a time when even the Savior feared death. But now no longer. He has triumphed over death; even His body has entered into the glory. The believer who abides in Christ as his full redemption, realizes even now his spiritual victory over death. It becomes to him the servant that removes the last rags of the old carnal vesture, here he be clothed upon with the new body of glory. It carries the body to the grave, to lie there as the seed whence the new body will arise the worthy companion of the glorified spirit. The resurrection of the body is no longer a barren doctrine, but a living expectation, and even an incipient experience, because the Spirit of Him that raised Jesus from the dead, dwells in the body as the pledge that even our mortal bodies shall be quickened.[3] This faith exercises its sanctifying influence in the willing surrender of the sinful members of the body to be mortified and completely subjected to the dominion of the Spirit, as preparation for the time when the frail body shall be changed and fashioned like to His glorious body.

This full redemption of Christ as extending to the body, has a depth of meaning not easily expressed. It was of man as a whole, soul and body that it is said that he was made in the image and likeness of God. In the angels, God had created spirits without material bodies; in the creation of the world, there was matter without spirit. Man was to be the highest specimen of divine art: the combination in one being, of matter and spirit in perfect harmony, as type of the most perfect union between God and

---

[3] *Rom.8:11-23 -*

His own creation. Sin entered in and appeared to thwart the divine plan: the material obtained a fearful supremacy over the spiritual. The Word was made flesh, the divine fulness received an embodiment in the humanity of Christ, that the redemption might be a complete and perfect one; that the whole creation, which now groaneth and travaileth in pain together, might be delivered from the bondage of corruption into the liberty of the glory of the children of God. God's purpose will not be accomplished, and Christ's glory will not be manifested fully, until the body, with that whole of nature of which it is part and head, has been transfigured by the power of the spiritual life, and made the transparent vesture for showing forth the glory of the Infinite Spirit. Then only shall we understand: "Christ Jesus is made unto us (complete) redemption."

Meantime we are taught to believe: "Of God are ye in Christ, as your redemption." This is not meant as a revelation, to be left to the future; for the full development of the Christian life, our present abiding in Christ must seek to enter into and appropriate it. We do this as we learn to triumph over death. We do it as we learn to look upon Christ as the Lord of our body, claiming its entire consecration, securing even here, if faith will claim it,[4] victory over the terrible dominion sin hath had in the body. We do this as we learn to look on all nature as part of the Kingdom of Christ, destined, even though it be through a baptism of fire, to partake in His redemption. We do it as we allow the powers of the coming world to possess us, and to lift us up into a life in the heavenly places, to enlarge our hearts and our views, to anticipate, even here, the things which have never entered into the heart of man to conceive.

Believer, abide in Christ as your redemption. Let this be the crown of your Christian life. Seek it not first or only, apart from the knowledge of Christ in His other relations. But seek it truly as that to which they are meant to lead you up. Abide in Christ as your redemption. Nothing will fit you for this but faithfulness in the previous steps of the Christian life. Abide in Him as your wisdom, the perfect revelation of all that God is and has for you. Follow, in the daily ordering of the inner and the outer life, with meek docility His teaching, and you shall be counted worthy to have secrets revealed to you which to most disciples are a sealed book. The wisdom will lead you into the mysteries of complete redemption.

---

[4] *Mark 16:17-18 -*

Abide in Him as your righteousness, and dwell clothed upon with Him in that inner sanctuary of the Father's favor and presence to which His righteousness gives you access. As you rejoice in your reconciliation, you shall understand how it includes all things, and how they too wait the full redemption; "for it pleased the Father by Him to reconcile all things unto Himself; by Him, I say, whether they be things on earth or things in heaven." And abide in Him as your sanctification; the experience of His power to make you holy, spirit and soul and body, will quicken your faith in a holiness that shall not cease its work until the bells of the horses and every pot in Jerusalem shall be holiness to the Lord. Abide in Him as your redemption, and live, even here, as the heir of the future glory. And as you seek to experience in yourself to the full, the power of His saving grace, your heart shall be enlarged to realize the position man has been destined to occupy in the universe, as having all things made subject to him, and you shall for your part be fitted to live worthy of that high and heavenly calling.

As *your* Righteousness

Of God are ye in Christ Jesus, who was made unto us wisdom from God, both righteousness and sanctification, and redemption.[5]

The first of the great blessings which Christ our wisdom reveals to us as prepared in Himself, is righteousness. It is not difficult to see why this must be first.

There can be no real prosperity or progress in a nation, a home, or a soul, unless there be peace. As not even a machine can do its work unless it be in rest, secured on a good foundation, quietness and assurance are indispensable to our moral and spiritual wellbeing. Sin had disturbed all our relations; we were out of harmony with ourselves, with men, and with God. The first requirement of a salvation that should really bring blessedness to us was peace. And peace can only come with right. Where everything is as God would have it, in God's order and in harmony with His will, there alone can peace reign. Jesus Christ came to restore peace on earth, and peace in the soul, by restoring righteousness. Because He is Melchizedek, King of righteousness, He reigns as King of Salem, King of peace.[6] He so fulfils the promise the prophets held out: "A king shall reign in righteousness: and the work of righteousness shall be peace, and the effect of righteousness, quietness and assurance forever."[7] Christ is made of God unto us righteousness; of God we are in Him as our righteousness; we are made the righteousness of God in Him. Let us try to understand what this means.

When first the sinner is led to trust in Christ for salvation, he, as a rule, looks more to His work than His person.

As he looks at the Cross, and Christ suffering there, the Righteous One for the unrighteous, he sees in that atoning death the only but sufficient foundation for his faith in God's pardoning mercy. The substitution, and the curse - bearing, and the atonement of Christ dying in the stead of sinners, are what give him peace. And as he understands

---

[5] *I Cor.1:30 -*
[6] *Heb.7:2 -*
[7] *Isa.32:1,17 -*

how the righteousness which Christ brings becomes his very own, and how, in the strength of that, he is counted righteous before God, he feels that he has what he needs to restore him to God's favor: "Being justified by faith, we have peace with God." He seeks to wear this robe of righteousness in the ever-renewed faith in the glorious gift of righteousness which has been bestowed upon him.

But as time goes on, and he seeks to grow in the Christian life, new needs arise. He wants to understand more fully how it is that God can thus justify the ungodly on the strength of the righteousness of another. He finds the answer in the wonderful teaching of Scripture as to the true union of the believer with Christ as the second Adam. He sees that it is because Christ had made Himself one with His people, and they were one with Him; that it was in perfect accordance with all law in the kingdom of nature and of heaven, that each member of the body should have the full benefit of the doing and the suffering as of the life of the head. And so, he is led to feel that it can only be in fully realizing his personal union with Christ as the Head, that he can fully experience the power of His righteousness to bring the soul into the full favor and fellowship of the Holy One. The work of Christ does not become less precious, but the Person of Christ more so; the work leads up into the very heart, the loss and the life of the Godman.

And this experience sheds its light again upon Scripture. It leads him to notice, what he had scarce remarked before, how distinctly the righteousness of God, as it becomes ours, is connected with the Person of the Redeemer. "This is His name whereby HE shall be called, JEHOVAH OUR RIGHTEOUSNESS." "IN JEHOVAH have I righteousness and strength." "OF God is HE made unto us righteousness." "That we might be made the righteousness of God IN HIM." "That I may be found IN HIM, having the righteousness of God." He sees how inseparable righteousness and life in Christ are from each other: "The righteousness of one comes upon all unto justification of life." "They which receive the gift of righteousness shall reign in life by one, Jesus Christ." And he understands what deep meaning there is in the key-word of the Epistle to the Romans: "The righteous shall live by faith." He is not now content with only thinking of the imputed righteousness as his robe; but, putting on Jesus Christ, and seeking to be wrapped up in, to be clothed upon with Himself and His life, he feels how completely the righteousness of God is his, because the Lord our righteousness is his. Before he understood this, he too often felt it difficult to wear his white robe all the day: it was as if he specially had to put it on when he came into God's presence to confess his sins and seek new grace. But now the living Christ Himself is his righteousness - that Christ who watches over and keeps and loves us as His own; it is no longer an impossibility to walk all the day enrobed in the loving presence with which He covers His people.

Such an experience leads still further. The life and the righteousness are inseparably linked, and the believer becomes more conscious than before of a righteous nature planted within him. The new man created in Christ Jesus, is "created in righteousness and true holiness." "He that doeth righteousness is righteous, even as He is righteous." The union to Jesus has effected a change not only in the relation to God, but in the personal state before God. And as the intimate fellowship to which the union has opened up the way is maintained, the growing renewal of the whole being makes righteousness to be his very nature.

To a Christian who begins to see the deep meaning of the truth, "HE is made to us righteousness," it is hardly necessary to say, "Abide in Him." As long as he only thought of the righteousness of the substitute, and our being counted judicially righteous for His sake, the absolute necessity of abiding in Him was not apparent. But as the glory of "Jehovah our righteousness" unfolds to the view, he sees that abiding in Him personally is the only way to stand, at all times, complete and accepted before God, as it is the only way to realize how the new and righteous nature can be strengthened from Jesus our Head. To the penitent sinner the chief thought was the righteousness which comes through Jesus dying for sin; to the intelligent and advancing believer, Jesus, the Living One, through whom the righteousness comes, is everything, because having Him he has the righteousness too.

Believer, abide in Christ as your righteousness. You bear about with you a nature altogether corrupt and vile, ever seeking to rise up and darken your sense of acceptance, and of access to unbroken fellowship with the Father. Nothing can enable you to dwell and walk in the light of God, without even the shadow of a cloud between, but the habitual abiding in Christ as your righteousness. To this you are called. Seek to walk worthy of that calling. Yield yourself to the Holy Spirit to reveal to you the wonderful grace that permits you to draw nigh to God, clothed in a divine righteousness. Take time to realize that the King's own robe has indeed been put on, and that in it you need not fear entering His presence. It is the token that you are the man whom the King delights to honor. Take time to remember that as much as you need it in the palace, no less do you require it when He sends you forth into the world, where you are the King's messenger and representative. Live your daily life in the full consciousness of being righteous in God's sight, an object of delight and pleasure in Christ. Connect every view you have of Christ in His other graces with this first one: "Of God He is made to your righteousness." This will keep you in perfect peace. Thus, shall you enter into, and dwell in, the rest of God. So, shall your inmost being be transformed into being righteous and doing righteousness. In your heart and life, it will become manifest where you dwell; abiding in Jesus Christ, the Righteous One, you will share His position, His character, and His blessedness: "Thou lovest righteousness, and hatest iniquity: therefore God, thy God, hath anointed thee with the oil of gladness above thy fellows." Joy and gladness above measure will be your portion.

As *your* Sanctification

*Of God are ye in Christ Jesus, who has made unto us
wisdom from God, both righteousness and sanctification,
and redemption.*[8]

"**P**aul unto the Church of God which is at Corinth to them
that are sanctified in Christ Jesus, called to be saints";
thus, the chapter opens in which we are taught that
Christ is our sanctification. In the Old Testament,
believers were called the righteous; in the New Testament they are called
saints, the holy ones, sanctified in Christ Jesus. Holy is higher than
righteous. I Holy in God has reference to His inmost being; righteous, to
His dealings with His creatures. In man, righteousness is but a stepping
stone to holiness. It is in this he can approach most near to the perfection
of God.[9] In the Old Testament righteousness was found, while holiness
was only typified; ill Jesus Christ, the Holy One, and in His people, His
saints or holy ones, it is first realized.

As in Scripture, and in our text, so in personal experience
righteousness precedes holiness. When first the believer finds Christ as
his righteousness, he has such joy in the new-made discovery that the
study of holiness hardly has a place. But as he grows, the desire for
holiness makes itself felt, and he seeks to know what provision his God
has made for supplying that need. A superficial acquaintance with God's
plan leads to the view that while justification is God's work, by faith in
Christ, sanctification is our work, to be performed under the influence of
the gratitude we feel for the deliverance we have experienced, and by the
aid of the Holy Spirit. But the earnest Christian soon finds how little
gratitude can supply the power. When he thinks that more prayer will
bring it, he finds that, indispensable as prayer is, it is not enough. Often
the believer struggles hopelessly for years, until he listens to the teaching
of the Spirit, as He glorifies Christ again, and reveals Christ, our
sanctification, to be appropriated by faith alone.

---

[8] *I Cor.1:30 -*
[9] *Matt.5:48; I Pet.1:16 -*

Christ is made of God unto us sanctification. Holiness is the very nature of God, and that alone is holy which God takes possession of and fills with Himself. God's answer to the question, How could sinful man become holy? is, "Christ, the Holy One of God." In Him, whom the Father sanctified and sent into the world, God's holiness was revealed incarnate, and brought within reach of man. "I sanctify myself for them, that they also may be sanctified in truth." There is no other way of our becoming holy, but by becoming partakers of the holiness of Christ.' And there is no other way of this taking place than by our personal spiritual union with Him, so that through His Holy Spirit His holy life flows into us. "Of God are ye in Christ, who is made unto us sanctification." Abiding by faith in Christ our sanctification is the simple secret of a holy life. The measure of sanctification will depend on the measure of abiding in Him; as the soul learns wholly to abide in Christ, the promise is increasingly fulfilled: "The very God of peace sanctify you wholly."

To illustrate this relation between the measure of the abiding and the measure of sanctification experienced, let us think of the grafting a tree, that instructive symbol of our union to Jesus. The illustration is suggested by the Savior's words, "Make the tree good, and his fruit good." I can graft a tree so that only a single branch bears good fruit, while many of the natural branches remain, and bear their old fruit - a type of believer in whom a small part of the life is sanctified, but in whom, from ignorance or other reasons, the carnal life still in many respects has full dominion. I can graft a tree so that every branch is cut off, and the whole tree becomes renewed to bear good fruit; and yet, unless I watch over the tendency of the stems to give sprouts, they may again rise and grow strong, and, robbing the new graft of the strength it needs, make it weak. Such are Christians who, when apparently powerfully converted, forsake all to follow Christ, and yet after a time, through unwatchfulness, allow old habits to regain their power, and whose Christian life and fruit are but feeble. But if I want a tree wholly made good, I take it when young, and, cutting the stem clean off on the ground, I graft it just where it emerges from the soil. I watch over every bud which the old nature could possibly put forth, until the flow of sap from the old roots into the new stem is so complete, that the old life has, as it were, been entirely conquered and covered by the new. Here I have a tree entirely renewed-emblem of the Christian who has learnt in entire consecration to surrender everything for Christ, and in a wholehearted faith wholly to abide in Him.

If, in this last case, the old tree were a reasonable being that could co-operate with the gardener, what would his language be to it? Would it not be this: "Yield now yourself entirely to this new nature with which I have invested you; repress every tendency of the old nature to give buds or sprouts; let all your sap and all your life-powers rise up into this graft from yonder beautiful tree, which I have put on you; so shall you bring forth sweet and much fruit." And the language of the tree to the gardener would be: "When you graft me, O spare not a single branch; let everything of the old self, even the smallest bud, be destroyed, that I may no longer live in my own, but in that other life that was cut off and brought and put upon me, that I might be wholly new and good." And, once again, could you afterwards ask the renewed tree, as it was bearing abundant fruit, what it could say of itself, its answer would be this: "In me, that is, in my roots, there dwells no good thing. I am ever inclined to evil; the sap I collect from the soil is in its nature corrupt, and ready to show itself in bearing evil fruit. But just when the sap rises into the sunshine to ripen into fruit, the wise gardener has clothed me with a new life, through which my sap is purified, and all my powers are renewed to the bringing forth of good fruit. I have only to abide in that which I have received. He cares for the immediate repression and removal of every bud which the old nature still would put forth."

Christian, fear not to claim God's promises to make you holy. Listen not to the suggestion that the corruption of your old nature would render holiness an impossibility. In your flesh dwells no good thing, and that flesh, though crucified with Christ, is not yet dead, but will continually seek to rise and lead you to evil. But the Father is the Husbandman. He has grafted the life of Christ on your life. That holy life is mightier than your evil life; under the watchful care of the Husbandman, that new life can keep down the workings of the evil life within you. The evil nature is there, with its unchanged tendency to rise up and show itself. But the new nature is there too - the living Christ, your sanctification, is there and through Him all your powers can be sanctified as they rise into life, and be made to bear fruit to the glory of the Father.

And now, if you would live a holy life, abide in Christ your sanctification. Look upon Him as the Holy One of God, made man that

He might communicate to us the holiness of God. Listen when Scripture teaches that there is within you a new nature, a new man, created in Christ Jesus in righteousness and true holiness. Remember that this holy nature which is in you is singularly fitted for living a holy life, and performing all holy duties, as much so as the old nature is for doing evil. Understand that this holy nature within you has its root and life in Christ in heaven and can only grow and become strong as the intercourse between it and its source is uninterrupted. And above all, believe most confidently that Jesus Christ Himself delights in maintaining that new nature within you, and imparting to it His own strength and wisdom for its work. Let that faith lead you daily to the surrender of all self-confidence, and the confession of the utter corruption of all there is in you by nature. Let it fill you with a quiet and assured confidence that you are indeed able to do what the Father expects of you as His child, under the covenant of His grace, because you have Christ strengthening you. Let it teach you to lay yourself and your services on the altar as spiritual sacrifices, holy and acceptable in His sight, a sweet-smelling savor. Look not upon a life of holiness as a strain and an effort, but as the natural outgrowth of the life of Christ within you. And let ever again a quiet, hopeful, gladsome faith hold itself assured that all you need for a holy life will most assuredly be given you out of the holiness of Jesus. Thus, will you understand and prove what it is to abide in Christ our sanctification.

NOTE

The thought that in the personal holiness of our Lord a new holy nature was formed to be communicated to us, and that we make use of it by faith, is the central idea of Marshall's invaluable work, The Gospel Mystery of Sanctification:

"One great mystery is, that the holy frame and disposition whereby our souls are furnished and enabled for immediate practice of the law, must be obtained by receiving it out of Christ's fulness, as a thing already prepared and brought to an existence ,for us in Christ, and treasured up in Him; and that, as we are justified by a righteousness wrought out in Christ, and imputed to us, so we are sanctified by such an holy frame and qualification as are first wrought out and completed in Christ for us, and then imparted to us. As our natural corruption was produced originally in the first Adam, and propagated from him to us, so our new nature and holiness is first produced in Christ, and derived from Him to us, or, as it were, propagated. So that we are not at all to work together with Christ in making or producing that holy frame in us, but only to take it to ourselves, and use it in our holy practice, as made ready to our hands. Thus, we have fellowship with Christ, in receiving that holy frame of spirit that was originally in Him; for fellowship is where several persons have the same things in common. This mystery is so great, that notwithstanding all the light of the Gospel, we commonly think that we must get a holy frame by producing it anew in ourselves, and by pursuing it and working it out of our own heart."

As *your* Strength

All power is given UNTO ME in heaven and in earth. [10]

Be strong IN THE LORD, and in the power of his might. [11]

My power is made perfect in weakness. [12]

There is no truth more generally admitted among earnest Christians than that of their utter weakness. There is no truth more generally misunderstood and abused. Here, as elsewhere, God's thoughts are heaven - high above man's thoughts.

The Christian often tries to forget his weakness: God wants us to remember it, to feel it deeply. The Christian wants to conquer his weakness and to be freed from it: God wants us to rest and even rejoice in it. The Christian mourns over his weakness: Christ teaches His servant to say, "I take pleasure in infirmities; most gladly will I glory in my infirmities." The Christian thinks his weakness his greatest hindrance in the life and service of God: God tells us that it is the secret of strength and success. It is our weakness, heartily accepted and continually realized, that gives us our claim and access to the strength of Him who has said, "My strength is made perfect in weakness."

When our Lord was about to take His seat upon the throne, one of His last words was: "All power is given unto me in heaven and on earth." Just as His taking His place at the right hand of the power of God was something new and true - a real advance in the history of the God-man - so was this clothing with all power. Omnipotence was now entrusted to the man Christ Jesus, that from henceforth through the channels of human nature it might put forth its mighty energies. Hence, He connected with this revelation of what He was to receive, the promise of the share that His disciples would have in it: When I am ascended, ye shall receive power from on high. [13] It is in the power of the omnipotent Savior that the believer must find his strength for life and for work.

---

[10] *MATT.28:18 -*

[11] *EPH.6.10 -*

[12] *2 COR.12:9 -*

[13] *Luke xxiv. 49; Acts i. 8 -*

It was thus with the disciples. During ten days they worshipped and waited at the footstool of His throne. They gave expression to their faith in Him as their Savior, to their adoration of Him as their Lord, to their love to Him as their Friend, to their devotion and readiness to work for Him as their Master. Jesus Christ was the one object of thought, of love, of delight. In such worship of faith and devotion their souls grew up into intensest communion with Him upon the throne, and when they were prepared, the baptism of power came. It was power within and power around.

The power came to qualify for the work to which they had yielded themselves - of testifying by life and word to their unseen Lord. With some the chief testimony was to be that of a holy life, revealing the heaven and the Christ from whom it came. The power came to set up the Kingdom within them, to give them the victory over sin and self, to fit them by living experience to testify to the power of Jesus on the throne, to make men live in the world as saints. Others were to give themselves up entirely to the speaking in the naive of Jesus. But all needed and all received the gift of power, to prove that now Jesus had received the Kingdom of the Father, all power in heaven and earth was indeed given to Him, and by Him imparted to His people just as they needed it, whether for a holy life or effective service. They received the gift of power, to prove to the world that the Kingdom of God, to which they professed to belong, was not in word but in power. By having power within, they had power without and around. The power of God was felt even by those who would not yield themselves to it. [14]

And what Jesus was to these first disciples, He is to us too. Our whole life and calling as disciples find their origin and their guarantee in the words: "All power is given to me in heaven and on earth." What He does in and through us, He does with almighty power. What He claims or demands, He works Himself by that same power. All He gives, He gives with power. Every blessing He bestows, every promise He fulfils, every grace He works-all, all is to be with power. Everything that comes from this Jesus on the throne of power is to bear the stamp of power. The weakest believer may be confident that in asking to be kept from sin, to grow in holiness, to bring forth much fruit, be may count upon these his

---

[14] *Acts 2.43; 4:13; 5:13 -*

petitions being fulfilled with divine power. The power is in Jesus; Jesus is ours with all His fulness; it is in us His members that the power is to work and be made manifest.

And if we want to know how the power is bestowed, the answer is simple: Christ gives His power in us by giving His life in us. He does not, as so many believers imagine, take the feeble life He finds in them, and impart a little strength to aid them in their feeble efforts. No; it is in giving His own life in us that He gives us His power. The Holy Spirit came down to the disciples direct from the heart of their exalted Lord, bringing down into them the glorious life of heaven into which He had entered. And so, His people are still taught to be strong in the Lord and in the power of His might. When He strengthens them, it is not by taking away the sense of feebleness and giving in its place the feeling of strength. By no means. But in a very wonderful way leaving and even increasing the sense of utter impotence, He gives them along with it the consciousness of strength in Him. "We have this treasure in earthen vessels, that the excellency of the power may be of God and not of us." The feebleness and the strength are side by side; as the one grows, the other too, until they understand the saying, "When I am weak, then am I strong; I glory in my infirmities, that the power of Christ may rest on me."

The believing disciple learns to look upon Christ on the throne, Christ the Omnipotent, as his life. He studies that life in its infinite perfection and purity, in its strength and glory; it is the eternal life dwelling in a glorified man. And when he thinks of his own inner life, and longs for holiness, to live well pleasing unto God, or for power to do the Father's work, he looks up, and, rejoicing that Christ is his life, he confidently reckons that that life will work mightily in him all he needs. In things little and things great, in the being kept from sin from moment to moment for which he has learned to look, or in the struggle with some special difficulty or temptation, the power of Christ is the measure of his expectation. He lives a most joyous and blessed life, not because he is no longer feeble, but because, being utterly helpless, he consents and expects to have the mighty Savior work in him.

The lessons these thoughts teach us for practical life are simple, but very precious. The first is, that all our strength is in Christ, laid up and waiting for use. It is there as an almighty life, which is in Him for us, ready to flow in according to the measure in which it finds the channels open. But whether its flow is strong or feeble, whatever our experience of it be, there it is in Christ: All power in heaven and earth. Let us take time to study this. Let us get our minds filled with the thought: That Jesus might be to us a perfect Savior; the Father gave Him all power. That is the qualification that fits Him for our needs: All the power of heaven over all the powers of earth, over every power of earth in our heart and life too.

The second lesson is: This power flows into us as we abide in close union with Him. When the union is feeble, little valued or cultivated, the inflow of strength will be feeble. When the union with Christ is rejoiced in as our highest good, and everything sacrificed for the sake of maintaining it, the power will work: "His strength will be made perfect in our weakness." Our one care must therefore be to abide in Christ as our strength. Our one duty is to be strong in the Lord, and in the power of His might. Let our faith cultivate large and clear apprehensions of the exceeding greatness of God's power in them that believe, even that power of the risen and exalted Christ by which He triumphed over every enemy.[15] Let our faith consent to Gods wonderful and most blessed arrangement: nothing but feebleness in us as our own, all the power in Christ, and yet within our reach as surely as if it were in us. Let our faith daily go out of self and its life into the life of Christ, placing our whole being at His disposal for Him to work in us. Let our faith, above all, confidently rejoice in the assurance that He will in very deed, with His almighty power, perfect His work in us. As we thus abide in Christ, the Holy Spirit, the Spirit of His power, will work mightily in us, and we too shall sing, "JEHOVAH is my strength and song: IN JEHOVAH I have righteousness and strength." "I can do all things through Christ, which strengtheneth me."

---

[15] *Eph. 1: 19-21 -*

As *your* Wisdom

Of God are ye in Christ Jesus, who was made unto us wisdom from God, both righteousness and sanctification, and redemption. [16]

Jesus Christ is not only Priest to purchase, and King to secure, but also Prophet to reveal to us the salvation which God bath prepared for them that love Him. Just as at the creation the light was first called into existence, that in it all God's other works might have their life and beauty, so in our text wisdom is mentioned first as the treasury in which are to be found the three precious gifts that follow. The life is the light of man; it is in revealing to us and making us behold the glory of God in His own face, that Christ makes us partakers of eternal life. It was by the tree of knowledge that sin came; it is through the knowledge that Christ gives that salvation comes. He is made of God unto us wisdom. In Him are hid all the treasures of wisdom and knowledge.

And of God you are in Him, and have but to abide in Him, to be made partaker of these treasures of wisdom. In Him you are, and in Him the wisdom is; dwelling in Him, you dwell in the very fountain of all light; abiding in Him, you have Christ the wisdom of God leading your whole spiritual life, and ready to communicate, in the form of knowledge, just as much as is needful for you to know. Christ is made unto us wisdom: you are in Christ.

It is this connection between what Christ has been made of God to us, and how we have it only as also being in Him, that we must learn to understand better. We shall thus see that the blessings prepared for us in Christ cannot be obtained as special gifts in answer to prayer apart from the abiding in Him. The answer to each prayer must come in the closer union and the deeper abiding in Him; in Him, the unspeakable gift, all other gifts are treasured up, the gift of wisdom and knowledge too.

How often have you longed for wisdom and spiritual understanding that you might know God better, whom to know is life eternal! Abide in

---

[16] *I COR.1:30* -

Jesus: your life in Him will lead you to that fellowship with God in which the only true knowledge of God is to be had. His love, His power, His infinite glory will, as you abide in Jesus, be so revealed as it hath not entered into the heart of man to conceive. You may not be able to grasp it with the understanding, or to express it in words; but the knowledge which is deeper than thoughts or words will be given - the knowing of God which comes of being known of Him. "We preach Christ crucified unto them which are called, Christ the power of God, and the wisdom of God."

Or you would fain count all things but loss for the excellency of the knowledge of Jesus Christ your Lord. Abide in Jesus and be found in Him. You shall know Him in the power of His resurrection and the fellowship of His sufferings. Following Him, you shall not walk in darkness, but have the light of life. It is only when God shines into the heart, and Christ Jesus dwells there, that the light of the knowledge of God in the face of Christ can be seen.

Or would you understand his blessed work, as He wrought it on earth, or works it from heaven by His Spirit? Would you know how Christ can become our righteousness, and our sanctification, and redemption? It is just as bringing, and revealing, and communicating these that He is made unto us wisdom from God. There are a thousand questions that at times come up, and the attempt to answer them becomes a weariness and a burden. It is because you have forgotten you are in Christ, whom God has made to be your wisdom. Let it be your first care to abide in Him in undivided fervent devotion of heart; when the heart and the life are right, rooted in Christ, knowledge will come in such measure as Christ's own wisdom sees meet. And without such abiding in Christ the knowledge does not really profit but is often most hurtful. The soul satisfies itself with thoughts which are but the forms and images of truth, without receiving the truth itself in its power. God's way is ever first to give us, even though it be but as a seed, the thing itself, the life and the power, and then the knowledge. Man seeks the knowledge first, and often, alas! never gets beyond it. God gives us Christ, and in Him hid the treasures of wisdom and knowledge. O let us be content to possess Christ, to dwell in Him, to make Him our life, and only in a deeper searching into Him, to search and find the knowledge we desire. Such knowledge is life indeed.

Therefore, believer, abide in Jesus as your wisdom, and expect from Him most confidently whatever teaching you may need for a life to the glory of the Father. In all that concerns your spiritual life, abide in Jesus as your wisdom. The life you have in Christ is a thing of infinite sacredness, far too high and holy for you to know how to act it out. It is He alone who can guide you, as by a secret spiritual instinct, to know what is becoming your dignity as a child of God, what will help and what will hinder your inner life, and specially your abiding in Him. Do not think of it as a mystery or a difficulty you must solve. Whatever questions come up as to the possibility of abiding perfectly and uninterruptedly in Him, and of really obtaining all the blessing that comes from it, always remember: He knows, all is perfectly clear to Him, and He is my wisdom. Just as much as you need to know and are capable of apprehending, will be communicated, if you only trust Him. Never think of the riches of wisdom and knowledge hid in Jesus as treasures without a key, or of your way as a path without a light. Jesus your wisdom is guiding you in the right way, even when you do not see it.

In all your intercourse with the blessed Word, remember the same truth: abide in Jesus, your wisdom. Study much to know the written Word; but study more to know the living Word, in whom you are of God. Jesus, the wisdom of God, is only known by a life of implicit confidence and obedience. The words He speaks are spirit and life to those who live in Him. Therefore, each time you read, or hear, or meditate upon the Word, be careful to take up your true position. Realize first your oneness with Him who is the wisdom of God; know yourself to be under His direct and special training; go to the Word abiding in Him, the very fountain of divine light - in His light you shall see light.

In all your daily life its ways and its work, abide in Jesus as your wisdom. Your body and your daily life share in the great salvation: in Christ, the wisdom of God, provision has been made for their guidance too. Your body is His temple, your daily life the sphere for glorifying Him: it is to Him a matter of deep interest that all your earthly concerns should be guided aright. Only trust His sympathy, believe His love, and wait for His guidance - it will be given. Abiding in Him, the mind will be calmed and freed from passion, the judgment cleared and strengthened, the light of heaven will shine on earthly things, and your prayer for wisdom, like Solomon's, will be fulfilled above what you ask or think.

And so, especially in any work you do for God, abide in Jesus as your wisdom. "We are created in Christ Jesus unto good works, which God bath before ordained that we should walk in them"; let all fear or doubt lest we should not know exactly what these works are, be put far away. In Christ we are created for them: He will show us what they are, and how to do them. Cultivate the habit of rejoicing in the assurance that the divine wisdom is guiding you, even where you do not yet see the way.

All that you can wish to know is perfectly clear to Him. As Man, as Mediator, He has access to the counsels of Deity, to the secrets of Providence, in your interest, and on your behalf. If you will but trust Him fully, and abide in Him entirely, you can be confident of having unerring guidance.

Yes, abide in Jesus as your wisdom. Seek to maintain the spirit of waiting and dependence, that always seeks to learn, and will not move but as the heavenly light leads on. Withdraw yourself from all needless distraction, close your ears to the voices of the world, and be as a docile learner, ever listening for the heavenly wisdom the Master has to teach. Surrender all your own wisdom; seek a deep conviction of the utter blindness of the natural understanding in the things of God; and both as to what you have to believe and have to do, wait for Jesus to teach and to guide. Remember that the teaching and guidance come not from without: it is by His life in us that the divine wisdom does His work. Retire frequently with Him into the inner chamber of the heart, where the gentle voice of the Spirit is only heard if all be still. Hold fast with unshaken confidence, even in the midst of darkness and apparent desertion, His own assurance that He is the light and the leader of His own. And live, above all, day by day in the blessed truth that, as He Himself, the living Christ Jesus, is your wisdom, your first and last care must ever be this alone - to abide in Him. Abiding in Him, His wisdom will come to you as the spontaneous outflowing of a life rooted in Him. I am, I abide in Christ, who was made unto us wisdom from God; wisdom will be given me.

Also available from this author: